LEGO STAR WARS

FALL OF THE JEDI

CONTENTS

INTRODUCTION

One of the wisest and most powerful groups in the galaxy, the Jedi Order are noble protectors of the Republic. They uphold justice during times of peace, and defend the Republic during the Clone Wars.

Yoda is the leader of the Jedi High Council and has accomplished many things over the course of his 900 years. He has commanded armies into battle. He has trained thousands of aspiring Jedi Knights. He has made great friends and dangerous foes.

From the golden days of the Galactic Republic to the chaos of the Clone Wars, the Jedi Order's influence on galactic events in the Republic is as important and far-reaching as the little Jedi Master Yoda himself.

This is the Jedi's story.

DATE OR DATES

Dates are fixed around the Battle of Yavin in year 0. The dates recorded in this book are measured in terms of years Before the Battle of Yavin (BBY), when the first Death Star was destroyed by Luke Skywalker and the Rebel Alliance.

PATH OF KNOWLEDGE

Most Jedi receive training from Yoda as younglings but only a few are chosen as his official Padawan apprentices. As his students have become Masters and taught apprentices of their own, Yoda's teachings have been passed down through generations of Jedi.

WHO TAUGHT WHO?

YODA

COUNT DOOKU

LUKE SKYWALKER

KI-ADI-MUNDI

> CAN I BE EXCUSED, MASTER YODA? MY HEAD IS FULL.

QUI-GON JINN

OBI-WAN KENOBI

ANAKIN SKYWALKER

AHSOKA TANO

> SO IN A WAY, YODA TRAINED ME TOO!

HOBBIES

Yoda's life isn't all hard work and fighting. He also enjoys cooking and reading the latest Jedi periodicals.

YODA

YODA IS ONE of the greatest Jedi Masters ever known. His power with the Force and talent with a lightsaber are matched only by his vast wisdom and compassion. The Grand Master is always willing to teach those who have the patience to listen.

IN BATTLE

Many enemies underestimate Yoda because of his size and age. Little do they know that when he finally cuts loose, he becomes a leaping, bouncing, lightsaber-swinging blur of Jedi fighting skill!

> # "A JEDI MUST HAVE THE DEEPEST COMMITMENT, THE MOST SERIOUS MIND."
> YODA

DATA FILE

- **HOMEWORLD:** UNKNOWN
- **BIRTH DATE:** 896 BBY
- **RANK:** GRAND MASTER
- **TRAINED BY:** UNKNOWN
- **WEAPON:** GREEN-BLADED LIGHTSABER

.... Natural crystals create green blade

Tan outer robes and brown undershirt

PORTRAIT OF A JEDI
Yoda has a reptilian appearance, a wrinkled and bumpy forehead, long, pointed ears, and wispy gray hair on the back of his head. Like most Jedi, Yoda dresses in simple, durable robes.

Yoda can use the Force to draw his **lightsaber** from his robes into his hand. He is a **master** of the **Ataru** lightsaber form, which involves **Force leaps**, twirls, and twists.

TOOL OF THE TRADE
900-year-old Yoda walks with the aid of a wooden gimer stick. Not only can it double as a weapon, but Yoda also chews on it for a nutritious snack.

> SNEAK UP ON ME YOU CANNOT. SENSE YOU I CAN!

7

SMALL BUT MIGHTY

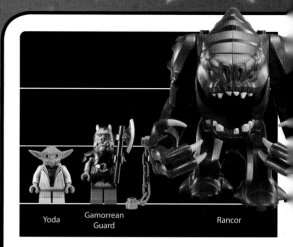

Yoda | Gamorrean Guard | Rancor

SMALL SIZE, BIG POWER
It's easy to underestimate Yoda. In most of the galaxy, the bigger something is, the tougher it is. But when it comes to a Jedi, what matters most is their ability to sense and channel the Force.

YODA MAY NOT be very tall, but what he lacks in height, he more than makes up for in power. His ability to channel the Force enables this aged Jedi Grand Master to leap great distances, perform acrobatic stunts, deflect weapon fire, and defeat his enemies in battle.

> UP YOUR SLEEVES, ANY MORE TRICKS DO YOU HAVE?

"SIZE MATTERS NOT. LOOK AT ME. JUDGE ME BY MY SIZE, DO YOU?"

YODA

Sith lightning

Floating Senate pod

FORCE PUSH

Thanks to his ability to push and pull objects using the Force, Yoda does not even need to lay his hands on his enemies to make them move out of his way. When Emperor Palpatine's guards try to stop him in the Senate building, Yoda has only to gesture —and they go flying!

WHOA! HOW DID HE DO THAT?

I DON'T KNOW, BUT I WISH I COULD DO IT, TOO!

Darth Sidious

HUH?! I CAN'T UNDERSTAND WHAT YOU'RE SAYING!

FORCE BUILDING

The Force binds everything in the galaxy together, but it can be used to take things apart as well. A highly Force-sensitive Jedi such as Yoda can use his powers to disassemble objects and rebuild them in different ways to make walls, cages, stairs, and even spaceships.

The Force is an invisible **energy** field that flows through every living being. Jedi are very **sensitive** to the **Force**. They spend years in deep **study** learning how to harness it in different ways.

FORCE DEFLECTION

Even without his lightsaber, Yoda is far from defenseless. He can use the Force to redirect all kinds of attacks—from blaster bolts and projectiles to the Force lightning wielded by Dark Lords of the Sith. When Darth Sidious hurls the deadly power of the dark side at him, Yoda simply catches it in his hands and gathers it up to throw back at him!

MACE WINDU

LEGENDARY JEDI MASTER Mace Windu is respected throughout the galaxy for his wisdom, courage, and skill with a lightsaber. Mace was the head of the Jedi Council before Yoda but he stepped down to lead troops in the Clone Wars.

A TRUSTED FRIEND

Mace is Yoda's second-in-command. When Yoda goes on an emergency rescue mission to Alderaan, Mace is the first Jedi he calls on for help. Mace and Yoda often trade wisdom and advice. They both sense Anakin Skywalker's strong emotional attachments and fear for the young Jedi's future.

Rare purple lightsaber blade

Jedi tunic

" THE OPPRESSION OF THE SITH WILL NEVER RETURN! "

MACE WINDU TO DARTH SIDIOUS

DATA FILE

- **HOMEWORLD:** HARUUN KAL
- **BIRTH DATE:** 72 BBY
- **RANK:** JEDI MASTER
- **TRAINED BY:** UNKNOWN
- **WEAPON:** PURPLE-BLADED LIGHTSABER

PALPATINE'S ARREST

Yoda respects Mace's loyalty and commitment to justice and the Jedi Order. When Mace learns that Supreme Chancellor Palpatine is a Sith Lord, he tries to arrest him. Unfortunately for Mace, his doubts about Anakin Skywalker prove to be correct. The young Jedi interferes in his duel against Palpatine and sides with the Sith.

Kit Fisto

I WILL DISASSEMBLE THE REPUBLIC!

Saesee Tiin

Agen Kolar

Chancellor Palpatine

NOT IF I DISASSEMBLE YOU FIRST!

Holoprojector

Bronzium statue

Mace Windu

Like **Yoda**, Mace prefers to resolve conflict through **negotiation**. But when the Jedi are forced into **war**, Mace doesn't hesitate to **fight** for the things he **believes** in.

BATTLE OF GEONOSIS

As the Clone Wars begin, Yoda and Mace come up with a two-part plan to start the Republic's droid Army on Geonosis. While Yoda goes to gather an army of clone troopers, Mace leads a strike force of Jedi Knights in a direct attack. During the battle, the master duelist faces and defeats infamous bounty hunter Jango Fett.

YODA THE TEACHER

IN HIS EIGHT CENTURIES of teaching, Yoda has instructed many Padawans, including some of the most famous Jedi of all time. Yoda is a natural teacher and is dedicated to providing generations of Padawans with the knowledge, skills, and attitude to become Jedi.

Holocrons project stories and information

Mechanical podium raises and lowers

HISTORY LESSON

The students in Yoda's classes do not always understand the meanings of his lectures at first. But as they grow older and wiser, they will come to appreciate their earliest lessons. One of the students' favorite classrooms is the Holocron Vault in the Jedi Temple, where they can watch holographic recordings from the long history of the Jedi Order.

YODA'S PADAWANS

New Jedi initiates are placed in clans that attend classes and training together. One of these is the Bear Clan, a group of brave younglings from different worlds. These young students have already had more adventures than many Jedi Knights twice their age.

WHAT MAKES A GOOD STUDENT?

Yoda requires more from his students than just great skill. Although young Anakin Skywalker is an excellent pilot with a very powerful connection to the Force, Yoda feels that his lateness to Jedi training and his overpowering emotions make him a poor candidate to become a Jedi.

THE ULTIMATE TEST

Yoda knows that no matter how well a student does at the Academy, the real test can be found only outside the safety of the Jedi Temple. When Anakin becomes the apprentice of Obi-Wan Kenobi, he risks his life chasing the shape-shifting bounty hunter Zam Wesell on Coruscant.

THIS IS MY FAVORITE LESSON SO FAR, MASTER!

Temporarily "borrowed" XJ-6 airspeeder

WELL, IT'S NOT MINE!

Claudite assassin
Zam Wesell

CHANCELLOR PALPATINE

YODA AND THE OTHER Jedi know Palpatine as the kindly Supreme Chancellor of the Galactic Republic. But Palpatine is secretly Darth Sidious—a Dark Lord of the Sith who steers events from behind the scenes to achieve his goal of controlling the galaxy.

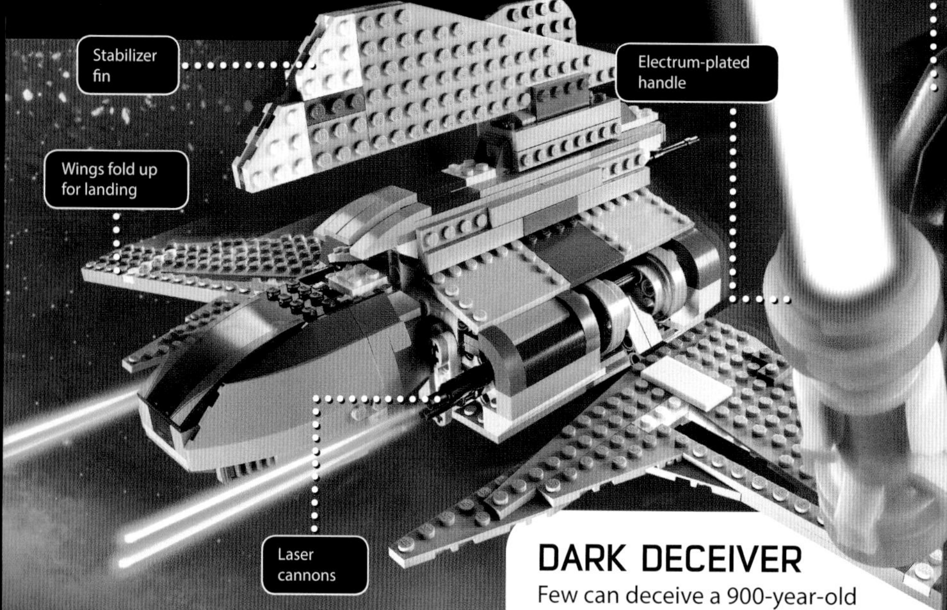

Formal Chancellor's garb

Stabilizer fin

Electrum-plated handle

Wings fold up for landing

Laser cannons

PALPATINE'S SHUTTLE
Officially, Palpatine's *Theta*-class T-2c shuttle carries him on Senate business. But it's also handy for sneaky escapes when his identity as Darth Sidious is about to be exposed.

DARK DECEIVER
Few can deceive a 900-year-old Jedi Master, but Palpatine is so strong in the dark side of the Force that not even Yoda suspects his true evil nature. He uses his cover to manipulate the Jedi, for example by giving them false information or sending them into Separatist traps.

"AREN'T YOU A LITTLE SMALL FOR A JEDI MASTER?"

"AS SHORT AS ME, YOUR REIGN WILL BE!"

RISE OF THE EMPEROR

When the pieces of his plan have come together, Palpatine betrays the Jedi and installs himself as Emperor of a new Galactic Empire. Seeing one last chance to confront the Sith Lord and restore peace to the galaxy, Yoda duels with him in the Senate building on Coruscant—but he is outmatched by the Emperor's rage and power.

Shadowy hood

Synthetic crystals create red blade

Face twisted by evil

Black Sith robes

DARK SIDE AGENTS

Palpatine uses others to do his dirty work while he keeps his distance and maintains his cover.

DARTH MAUL
Yoda realizes the Sith have returned when Darth Sidious's apprentice strikes on Tatooine.

ASAJJ VENTRESS
Wielding twin lightsabers, this Jedi-trained Nightsister goes on missions for the Separatists, often coming up against Yoda.

SAVAGE OPRESS
...be only two Sith at a time, the ranks of the dark side expand with warriors including Darth Maul's brutal brother.

DATA FILE

- HOMEWORLD: NABOO
- BIRTH DATE: 82 BBY
- RANK: SUPREME CHANCELLOR
- TRAINED BY: DARTH PLAGUEIS
- WEAPON: RED-BLADED LIGHTSABER, FORCE LIGHTNING

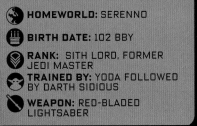

- **HOMEWORLD:** SERENNO
- **BIRTH DATE:** 102 BBY
- **RANK:** SITH LORD, FORMER JEDI MASTER
- **TRAINED BY:** YODA FOLLOWED BY DARTH SIDIOUS
- **WEAPON:** RED-BLADED LIGHTSABER

COUNT DOOKU

TO YODA AND MOST of the galaxy, Count Dooku is the head of the Separatists, a nobleman and former Jedi who leads the attack against the Republic. But like his master Palpatine, Dooku leads a double life—as the Sith apprentice Darth Tyranus.

JEDI TURNCOAT

When Dooku was a Jedi Padawan, he learned the art of lightsaber combat from Yoda himself. That is how he knows of the Kyber crystals hidden in the lightsabers of Yoda's pupils—and how Yoda realizes that his former student is responsible when they are stolen by General Grievous.

Royal tunic lined with armorweave

Curved-hilt lightsaber

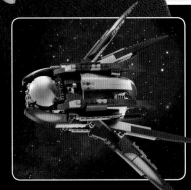

SOLAR SAILER

Dooku's Geonosian *Punworcca 116*-class interstellar sloop has a solar sail that propels it silently through space.

STUDENT VS. MASTER

When Yoda and Dooku confront each other during the first battle of the Clone Wars, the Count has grown strong in the dark side of the Force. But as the teacher and his former Padawan duel with Force powers and lightsaber blades, it quickly becomes clear that Yoda is still the master.

> WHEN LAST WE MET, I WAS BUT THE LEARNER ...

> THE WRONG MOVIE, THAT IS!

Having **lost** Dooku to the **dark side**, Yoda works hard to make sure his younglings understand the difference between **right** and **wrong**.

PLAN FOR DOMINATION

Dooku's talent with a lightsaber is rivaled only by his intelligence and cunning. His knowledge of technology aids him in his scheme for the stolen Kyber crystals. He plans to use them to build an army of loyal Force-enhanced clone warriors to fight alongside the Sith—starting with Jek-14!

A SPEEDY GETAWAY

Like any good villain, Dooku knows when to stand and fight, and when it's better to turn tail and run. If the odds are against him, he hops on his modified Flitknot speeder and flees to safety.

Geonosian design

Stabilizer fins

YODA THE GRAND MASTER

LONG HOURS, THIS JOB HAS ... BUT LOOKING FORWARD TO RETIRING ON A SWAMP PLANET, I AM NOT!

LEGENDARY LEADER

To become Grand Master, a Jedi must receive a unanimous vote from the entire Jedi Council and display the highest degree of wisdom, skill, and responsibility. During the Clone Wars, Yoda has to lead his fellow Jedi in both peace and battle.

SAESEE TIIN

A horned, telepathic Iktotchi, Saesee Tiin is an important member of the Jedi Council. He is a brave soldier and celebrated starfighter pilot. Tiin's mind-reading abilities give him a natural advantage in both space and lightsaber combat.

KI-ADI-MUNDI

As a Cerean, Ki-Adi-Mundi has a binary brain in his large head that helps him to focus on multiple tasks at the same time. Unlike most Jedi, he joined the Council as a Knight before reaching the rank of Master.

KIT FISTO

Kit Fisto is an amphibious Nautolan who is equally at home in water and on land. His victories as a general in the Clone Wars lead to his appointment to the Jedi High Council—although he is too modest to accept at first!

SHAAK TI

Shaak Ti is a Togruta member of the Jedi Council. She often takes on missions of defense, whether rescuing captured allies, protecting new clone troopers on Kamino, or safeguarding the Jedi Temple from attack.

AGEN KOLAR

Like fellow Council member Eeth Koth, Agen Kolar is a Zabrak. Kolar prefers fighting to discussion and negotiation and is often the first to ignite his lightsaber. He is almost as good a duelist as the legendary Mace Windu.

YODA IS THE GRAND MASTER

of the Jedi Order, a position that holds great honor and respect. Yoda works alongside the wisest and most skilled Jedi on the Council. Together, they select other talented Jedi to undertake special missions, plan military strategies in times of war, and seek guidance from the Force.

THE JEDI COUNCIL

The Jedi High Council is made up of 12 exemplary Jedi Masters who are elected to guide the Jedi Order. The Council members meet in the Jedi Temple on Coruscant to discuss matters of importance to the Republic and to advise the Supreme Chancellor, the leader of the Republic.

EETH KOTH

When he was first brought before the High Council as a child, Eeth Koth was thought to be too old for Jedi training. Fortunately, the strong Force-user proved his worth and he has even gone on to serve on the Council himself.

EVEN PIELL

Jedi Council member Even Piell shows a fearlessness in battle that more than makes up for his small stature. The battle-worn Jedi's long Lannik ears give him super-sensitive hearing.

PLO KOON

A Jedi Council member of the Kel Dor species, Plo Koon has to wear a special mask to see and breathe when off his home planet. Koon has a strong sense of justice and is skilled at moving objects using the Force.

AAYLA SECURA

A Twi'lek Jedi Master, Aayla Secura has confronted and overcome the temptations of the dark side of the Force. She is intelligent and a talented lightsaber wielder, but she still retains a mischievous streak.

LUMINARA UNDULI

Mirialan Jedi Master Luminara Unduli leads her clone troopers alongside Yoda during the Battle of Kashyyyk. Her chin tattoos symbolize her dedication to constantly improving her physical skills.

BARRISS OFFEE

As Master Unduli's Padawan apprentice, Barriss Offee has already seen much of the chaos caused by warfare. That is why she has trained to be a Jedi healer. Her Mirialan facial tattoos signify her achievements as a healer.

GENERAL GRIEVOUS

YODA HAS RARELY faced an enemy as filled with hate as the savage cyborg Grievous. The terrifying Supreme Commander of the Separatist Droid Army delights in causing mayhem and trouble —especially for the Jedi.

Eyes from original body

Stolen Jedi lightsaber

Mask-like face plate

A MATCH FOR THE JEDI

Grievous was once an organic being, but he chose to be rebuilt as a cyborg after he almost died in a shuttle crash. He had always been jealous of the Jedi's abilities, and now his cyborg body would be strong enough to fight them. Even so, Grievous knows how powerful Yoda is, and prefers to avoid directly challenging the skilled Jedi Master

Duranium alloy body

Clawed feet

DATA FILE

🐾 **HOMEWORLD:** KALEE

🏛 **BIRTH DATE:** UNKNOWN

▽ **RANK:** SUPREME COMMANDER

🦂 **TRAINED BY:** COUNT DOOKU

🗡 **WEAPON:** BLASTER, LIGHTSABERS

What does a **wise** Jedi Master do when faced with an opponent with four whirling **lightsabers**? **Easy**—Yoda uses his lightsaber to **slice** the floor out from under his foe!

LIGHTSABERS

Grievous may not be Force-sensitive, but he is deadly with a lightsaber. His prized possession is his collection of Jedi lightsabers, each taken from a defeated foe. He's evil enough to even steal the lightsabers of Jedi Padawans.

Command bridge

Ion pulse cannon

The super-weapon is longer than four Republic *Venator*-class Star Destroyers.

THE *MALEVOLENCE*

A secret Separatist super-weapon, the *Malevolence* is one of General Grievous's flagships. It is armed with a pair of giant ion pulse cannons that can knock out the power of an entire Republic fleet.

Ion drive

ngle-pilot ckpit

DROID ARMY

mean he has to like them. His favorite hobby is shouting at his battle droids and ordering them into battle. And if Yoda and the other Jedi destroy the droids, then who cares? The Separatists can always make more.

Laser cannon

IEVOUS'S
ARFIGHTER

n personal touch, General evous makes use of his odified Belbullab-22 starfighter, e *Soulless One*. Its enhanced hyperdrive transports n swiftly across the galaxy as he carries out the sinister ns of Count Dooku and Darth Sidious.

YODA THE GENERAL

YODA DOES NOT like to use violence, but he will fight to defend the Republic and the Jedi Order. When the Clone Wars begin, he becomes the reluctant leader of Jedi generals and an army of clone troopers.

Firing proton torpedo

> HERE'S THE SHUTTLE. WHO CALLED FOR A LIFT?

Mace Windu

> ALL CLONES— ATTACK!

Clone trooper

Nu-class Republic attack shuttle

Commander Gree

> WE GET SWEET EXTRA GEAR, TOO!

Commander Cody

OFFICER CLASS
Many Jedi serve as generals of the Clone Army. The clone officers who report to the Jedi often distinguish themselves enough to receive their own unique nicknames and armor markings. Commander Cody of the 212th Attack Battalion sometimes accompanies Yoda on his missions.

GROUND FORCES

Along with standard vehicles such as wheeled and repulsorlift tanks, the Republic Army makes use of many different all-terrain walkers, from the fast and agile AT-RT to the massive six-legged AT-TE. These are operated by clone troopers, who are supported on the ground by Jedi generals.

> HEY, I CAN SEE MY HOUSE FROM UP HERE!

Armored panels protect driver

501

Blaster cannon

AT-RT (All Terrain Recon Transport)

Clone trooper

ARF (Advanced Recon Force) trooper

501st trooper

Clone pilot

> WHERE ARE THE REST OF YOU GUYS?

Jet trooper

Special Forces Commander

AIR FORCES

Clone-piloted flying vehicles deploy from enormous Republic cruisers in orbit over battleground planets. Heavily armed gunships carry troops and vehicles to the surface, while Republic attack shuttles and starfighters take on enemy ships in the skies and in space.

> SO WHEN DO I GET A PROMOTION TO COMMANDER!?

Commander Wolffe

Captain Rex

SPECIALIST CLONES

They may have identical faces under their helmets, but not every clone trooper is the same. Some receive training and equipment for special jobs, such as piloting vehicles, scouting hostile environments, and handling heavy weaponry. A few even have jetpacks!

23

HOW DOES YODA CHANGE THE COURSE OF A BATTLE?

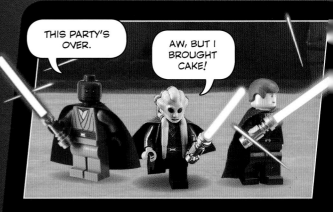

Double cockpits for pilot and co-pilot

Anti-personnel cannon

ON THE SCORCHED and dusty planet of Geonosis, the Jedi have fought bravely, but find themselves outnumbered by Count Dooku's Separatist battle droids. Just when all seems lost, Yoda arrives with a surprise: the Grand Army of the Republic. This force of armored clone troopers turns the tide of the battle and saves the day.

THIS PARTY'S OVER.

AW, BUT I BROUGHT CAKE!

JEDI IN TROUBLE
Force powers and the ability to block laser bolts with a lightsaber make a single Jedi more than a match for most opponents. But up against thousands of battle droids, even Mace Windu and his team need help. Without Yoda, the battle would be lost.

Troop bay

Composite-
beam pinpoint
laser turret

YODA TO THE RESCUE

The Jedi Master takes command of the clone army and directs his Republic gunships to aid the Jedi on Geonosis. Their arrival is a complete surprise to the Separatists, who thought they had beaten the Jedi. Yoda's army reinvigorates the Republic's fight and Count Dooku flees.

The **Republic gunship** is a familiar sight during the Clone Wars. Also known as Low Altitude Assault Transports (LAATs), these **powerful** ships transport dozens of **clone troopers** in their open central sections.

AGAINST THE SEPARATISTS

The Battle of Geonosis marks the beginning of the Clone Wars. Although the Jedi do not lose this battle, they have far from won the war. Under Yoda's expert leadership, the Republic army battles the Separatists all over the galaxy. On world after world, Yoda's wise strategies help the clone troopers and their Jedi generals to score important victories against the ever-expanding ranks of droid legions.

YOU KNOW WHAT TO DO.

Clone commander CC-1004, nicknamed "Gree"

Order 66 is a contingency plan for dealing with the **Jedi Order** should the Jedi ever become a **threat** to the Republic. When the clone troopers receive the Order 66 **command**, they betray their Jedi allies with **deadly** consequences.

WHEN WAS YODA'S DARKEST HOUR?

THE GREATEST BETRAYAL that Yoda ever faces comes when Supreme Chancellor Palpatine commands the Clone Army to turn on their Jedi generals. Most of the Jedi fall to the unexpected attack. Just a few scattered survivors remain, on the run from the forces of Emperor Palpatine's newly established Empire.

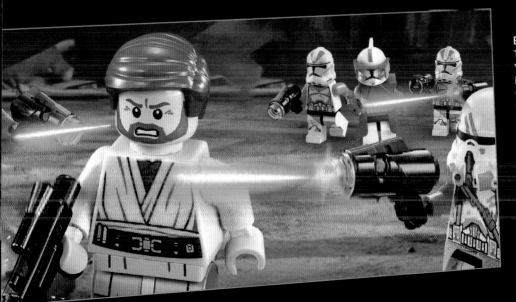

THIS JEDI IS IN BIG TROUBLE!

41st Elite Corps clone trooper

Holographic image of Palpatine

CLONE CRISIS

Yoda has relied on his clone troopers on dozens of planets during the Clone Wars, and he trusts them to always carry out their missions. During the Battle of Kashyyyk, Yoda knows that Commander Gree will faithfully follow his orders—he just doesn't realize whose orders the clone commander will follow first!

ORDER 66

As part of his plan to take over the galaxy, Supreme Chancellor Palpatine contacts the clone commanders and executes Order 66—a secret instruction that declares the Jedi to be traitors to the Republic. It is the beginning of a new regime and the fall of the old Jedi Order.

END OF AN ERA

Through the Force, Yoda senses the danger just in time and turns the tables on his would-be assassins. With the help of his Wookiee friends, Yoda flees Kashyyyk aboard a small escape pod. Obi-Wan Kenobi escapes a similar ambush on Utapau. They both meet on Coruscant, where Yoda decides to confront the new Emperor, and Obi-Wan prepares to stop Darth Vader.

GLOSSARY

BATTLE DROID
A Separatist robot designed for combat.

BOUNTY HUNTER
Someone who is hired to track down or destroy people or objects for money.

CHANCELLOR
The title given to the head of the Republic.

CLONE TROOPERS
Soldiers of the Republic Clone Army. They are identical because they share the same genes.

CLONE WARS
A series of galaxy-wide battles fought between the Republic's Clone Army and the Separatist Droid Army, which took place between 22 and 19 BBY.

CYBORG
A being that is partly a living organism and partly a robot.

DARK SIDE
The evil side of the Force that feeds off negative emotions.

DEATH STAR
An enormous Imperial battle station, which has enough firepower to destroy an entire planet.

DROID
A robot. Droids come in many shapes and sizes and serve a variety of duties.

EMPIRE
A tyrannical power that rules the galaxy under the leadership of Emperor Palpatine, a Sith Lord.

EMPEROR
Ruler of the Empire.

FORCE
The energy that flows through all living things. It can be used for good or evil.

FORCE-ENHANCED CLONE
A Force-powered clone created by Separatist leader and Sith apprentice Count Dooku.

FORCE LEAP
A huge jump made by someone using the Force to enhance their natural ability.

FORCE LIGHTNING
Deadly rays of blue energy used as a weapon.

FORCE PUSH
A blast of energy that a Force-user can use to knock over an opponent.

HOLOCRON
An ancient device that contains large amounts of data. It is activated through use of the Force.

JEDI
A member of the Jedi Order who studies the light side of the Force.

JEDI COUNCIL
Twelve senior Jedi who meet to make important decisions.

JEDI KNIGHT
A full member of the Jedi Order who has completed all of their training.

JEDI GRAND MASTER
The head of the Jedi Order and the greatest and wisest of the Jedi Masters.

JEDI MASTER
An experienced and high-ranking Jedi who has demonstrated great skill and dedication.

KYBER CRYSTAL
A very powerful crystal used in lightsabers. It greatly magnifies the powers of those who are sensitive to the Force.

LIGHTSABER
A sword-like weapon with a blade of pure energy that is used by Jedi and Sith.

LIGHT SIDE
The good side of the Force that brings peace and justice.

PADAWAN
A young Jedi apprentice who is in training to become a full-fledged Jedi Knight.

REBEL ALLIANCE
The organization that resists and fights the Empire.

REPUBLIC
The democratic government that rules many planets in the galaxy.

SENATE
The government of the Republic. It is made up of senators from all over the galaxy.

SENATOR
A person who acts as a representative for their planet in the Senate.

SEPARATISTS
An alliance of those who are opposed to the Republic.

SITH
An ancient sect of Force-sensitives who seek to use the dark side of the Force to gain power.

YOUNGLING
A Force-sensitive child who joins the Jedi Order to be trained in the Jedi arts.

DK | Penguin Random House

Senior Editors Elizabeth Dowsett
and Helen Murray
Editor Matt Jones
Senior Designer Lisa Sodeau
Designer Jon Hall
Senior DTP Designer David McDonald
Senior Producer Lloyd Robertson
Managing Editor Simon Hugo
Design Manager Guy Harvey
Creative Manager Sarah Harland
Art Director Lisa Lanzarini
Publisher Julie Ferris
Publishing Director Simon Beecroft

Additional photography by Gary Ombler

Dorling Kindersley would like to thank: Randi Sørensen and Louise Weiss
Borup at the LEGO Group; Jonathan W. Rinzler, Troy Alders, Rayne Roberts,
Pablo Hidalgo, and Leland Chee at Lucasfilm; Lisa Stock for editorial
assistance and John Goldsmid for design assistance.

First published in the United States in 2015 by
DK Publishing, 345 Hudson Street, New York, New York, 10014

Contains material previously published in
LEGO® Star Wars®: The Yoda Chronicles (2013)

002-284485-Feb/15

Page design copyright © 2015 Dorling Kindersley Limited
A Penguin Random House Company

A catalog record for this book is available from the Library of Congress.

ISBN: 978-5-0010-1299-3

Color reproduction by Alta Image, UK
Printed and bound in China

www.dk.com
www.LEGO.com/starwars

A WORLD OF IDEAS:
SEE ALL THERE IS TO KNOW